STEWART HENDERSON

Stewart Henderson was born in Liverpool in 1952. His collections of poetry include *Fan Male*, *Assembled in Britain*, and *A Giant's Scrapbook*, the last two having gone to several reprints. His poems feature in numerous publications, including several GCSE anthologies. He has fulfilled commissions for BBC Radio's 1, 2, 3 and 4; as well as for television on BBC1 and 2 and networked ITV.

Stewart performs his poetry extensively in the UK and abroad and his countless appearances have included the prestigious Lincoln Center for Performing Arts in New York, the Edinburgh Fringe, and the National Concert Hall, Dublin. He is also an experienced and accomplished interviewer. For over three years Stewart hosted *The Receiving End* at the Nave, Uxbridge, where his chosen guests included Sir Edward Heath, Germaine Greer, Michael Heseltine, Anita Roddick, Stephen Fry, Tony Benn and Melvyn Bragg. Also a published songwriter, in 1992 one of his songs reached the charts.

To our dear Ann
Our hearts are with you
in these fragile days. Thank
you deeply for your immense
support and encouragement,
and for your belief in us.
We head together to our Homeland,
and cherish the hope of reunion
with loved ones. All ours, Stewart & Carol

BY THE SAME AUTHOR

Poetry

General

HOMELAND

Stewart Henderson

Hodder & Stoughton
LONDON SYDNEY AUCKLAND

British Library Cataloguing in Publication Data

A catalogue record for this book is available from the British Library

ISBN 0-340-59118-8

Published by Hodder and Stoughton, a division of Hodder and Stoughton Limited, Mill Road, Dunton Green, Sevenoaks, Kent TN13 2YA. Editorial Office: 47 Bedford Square, London WC1B 3DP.

Photoset by Rowland Phototypesetting Limited, Bury St Edmunds, Suffolk

Printed in Great Britain by
Cox and Wyman Limited, Reading, Berks.

This book can only be for Carol:

Love has no enemies
for it has never declared war
Love breathes peace
and inspires meekness
Love is married to gentleness
and gives encouragement
Love walks the path of selflessness
and gathers beauty
And Love is you, my Love.

*   *   *

and for Maisie, who saw us through so much,
and gave us unconditional love. If Steinbeck
can write a book about a dog, then I can say
'thank you' to one, in a dedication.

ACKNOWLEDGMENTS

Some of the following poems were originally commissioned for television and live performance – notably the BBC TV series *Stop and Think, Christianity in Today's World*, and *Topics*; and the Tear Fund production *Broken Image*. I am particularly grateful to John Forrest and Stephen Rand in these contexts.

To others who have taken an encouraging interest in my work (including those who have performed it), and contributed friendship and support in so many ways, I extend my gratitude and appreciation. These would include:

David and Mary Brett; Revd Jim Brown and all our friends at Leadhills, especially Isabel and Roy Weir, and Tom and Sharon Dodgson; Bill and Marion Davidson; Eric Delve; Pete and Jen Etherton; Angus Jackson; Ethel Jefferyes; Bryan and Jenny Johnston; Mick and Annie Rock; Professor Grady Spires; Daf Thompson; and John and Sarah Webb.

I also want to thank my agent, Darley Anderson, for his invaluable advice, understanding and wise insights.

CONTENTS

Homeland

Travels

Fat Woman on the Sofa

HOMELAND

WE WATCHED THE SPRING AND THEN WE SLEPT

We watched the Spring
and then we slept;
as the gold gorse sparks
and the wild, wind-white swans nest
on the sparse, still shore,
two fallen clouds at rest.

We watched the Spring
and then we slept;
as the bracken,
browned before by Autumn's full fire;
receives now green blood
within its cracking pyre.

We watched the Spring
and then we slept;
as the hawk hangs
in heights of mist
then weaves
slow, scrolling circles
up towards heaven's eaves.

We watched the Spring
and then we slept;
as the gold gorse sparks
and the wild, wind-white swans nest
on the sparse, still shore,
two fallen clouds at rest.

CREDENTIALS OF LIBERTY

I knew dependency
I craved the teat
My robes of jewels and skies
became a smeared sheet

I breathed in cattle's breath
I lay near dung
I was a refugee with
an outsider's tongue

I slept amongst the rocks
where demons boast
I spent my final hours
stabbed to a post

My birth was destitute
My grave not mine
My death was toasted with
A rag of sour wine

I knew dependency
I cried in straw
I have the right to bring
Good news to the poor.

HOMELAND

'Do you see the mystery of our pain?
That we bear poverty
And are able to sing and dream sweet things'
                    Ben Okri – *African Elegy*

We're heading for a clearing
where the scrub is made of jade
it's a place of sweet aroma
where who we are is weighed
though none of us can walk it
and very few can crawl
we're on our way towards it
as we hear the Shofar call

We're heading for a clearing
where the trees burn up our sores
where the wild beasts lie before us
and there's just one lion that roars
and his mane is made of ermine
with eyelashes of lace
and he's stalked the vain and powerful
and he's snarling in their face

We're heading for a clearing
to a table where we'll feast
we'll be sitting next to Judah
though on earth we were the least
and our bellies won't be bloated
nor our eyes weep with disease

5

for we're heading to our Homeland
and we'll wander where we please

In our Homeland
In our Homeland
In our Homeland . . .

THE AIR IS FAR FROM SILENT

The air is far from silent
there is a song we cannot hear
it is the overture of planets
and the sound of stars
engraving themselves into space
We are lower than this
as we singe the sky
and stain the soil
with whims and experiments

The air is far from silent
it hums with the harmony of God
the tone is unimaginable
the descant is made of wings
as the mountains of mysterious moons
compose a chorus for a future recital
We do not know these notes
But the air is far from silent
and if we listen, there is even
the murmur of mansions being moulded.

LIMITED IMPRESSIONS

The First World War
was fought in black and white.
Men, who became absent grandfathers,
ran at each other in thick, unforgiving coats
across the hacked fields,
the starter's random gun ending
their tin-hat sprint,
and they suddenly slept.
Some who hurdled the barbed line
qualified for the next day's heats
as they wearily swayed
in long, damp hammocks of foul earth
smoking themselves through the churning, charcoal
  night.

The Second World War
was a thumbs-up affair
filmed by Pathé.
Virtually all who auditioned got a part.
Fledgling stunt men leapt into the sky's dim shades
sometimes landing in meadows that blew up.
There were other locations.
Bland beaches and exotic deserts,
where seedless fathers waded and scurried,
like khaki sand mice, after deaf tanks.
When the credits rolled at the end
there were so many names.

Today, understandably, we hide from wars,
nervously flicking channels
or phoning for pizza, whilst thinking

'Wars have a way of ruining things.
People bring wars on themselves.
We're past that stage.
Wars are for other times'.

WALL OF CONFLICT

In the patent-leather moonlight
under Heaven's chandelier
The foxtrot swirl of romance
paints a heady, frail veneer

Of harmony, deep passion
and the fireworks of embrace
But when the conquest's over
Will you still wear a sweet face?

So just in case your whispers
are the strokes of shallow care
I will give myself, in morsels,
and conceal my heart elsewhere.

For we are the Wall of Conflict
of enmity and spite,
a bricked-up, lonely universe
where 'I' is always right.

MISSING

God, being the Pastor
as well as Creator,
thought it not good
for Adam to be alone.

So He sculpted Eve.
With all His heart
He moulded her
and she breathed His breath.
And when she spoke
elephants and orchids listened.

Adam liked her, even loved her,
but then: looked past her
as he has forever.
When she needed comfort
he regarded her unclean
when she yearned with feelings
more brittle than skin,
he turned over and slept.
When they made love
it was quick,
sometimes silent,
a mute wake
an empty satisfaction,
and afterwards
she bathed alone.

I'M IN THE DARK WITH YOU

I tried to surround you
forgive me, I'm male
I'm a timid lounge lizard
who's just lost his tail
Now I'm in the dark with you.

I do tend to rush things
It's masculine drive
I'm Romeo on
a King's Cross 125
And I'm in the dark with you.

I'm completely unmoved
by a gloss centrefold
I'm thoroughly houseproud
a new man for old
But I'm still in the dark with you.

Nocturnal confusion,
the silence of doubt,
and how to avoid
being laddish throughout
When I'm here in the dark with you.

Maybe it's hormones, maybe it's fate,
it's certainly gender that gets us in this state
but now all I wish is to stay awake late
and be still, in the dark, with you.

COUNTER-BALANCE

This was how it was
before I dipped canaries in sunlight
and gave the water buffalo its rolling stroll
before the dolphin had told its first joke
not even the lion had yet leaped from his lair
This was how it was;
with My perfect Partners
We laid out the dance floor
opened up the ballroom of creation
hung planets as lanterns
and stars for concealed lighting.
Our choreography lasted light years
and our joy far longer.
Then We constructed a dressing room
We called it 'Earth'
It was pure, and it shone
And it smelled like Me.
In time, I employed a couple of attendants
and invited them
to come and make up a fivesome.
They were both so beautiful
But they refused
and started to make up their own
disjointed steps
as the dressing room faded into shadow.
And so I wrote My grief
over everything I had made
and pined for My two attendants.
One of My perfect Partners
even entered the dressing room
to invite them once again

to join Our unblemished company
They sent Him back
bloodied, pummelled, gored.
They were even going to break His legs
They thought that would stop Him dancing.
But that I would not allow
For it was His dancing
His pleading arabesque
that turned away My wrath
and lit up the deep darkness.

PRESS GANG

*The first 8 verses
are genuine tabloid headlines.
You read it here first.*

Madman Gets Away With Murder.
Soap Star Spills Her Saucy Past
Jilted Lover Bashes Wardrobe
Queen Mum Meets EastEnders Cast

Sick Fan Sends His Ear To Pop Star
Lefties Grab For Town Hall Jobs
Channel Tunnel Rabies Nightmare
Birch These Evil Soccer Yobs

Who's The Looniest World Leader?
Find Out In Our Readers' Poll
'Killer Dogs Love Kids' Claims Owner
Falklands Hero Claiming Dole

Wapping Coppers Cleared Of Charges
Shamed M.P. In City Con
Firebomb Ruins Asian Grocer
Slimming Star Puts Weight Back On

Visit Britain's Kindest Village
Spear Thrown During Night Club Raid
Spot The Balls And Win Five Million
Britain Cuts Back Third World Aid

Budgie Swears At Tax Inspector
Pilot Caused Collision Jet
Bishops Blamed For Nation's Morals
Credit Card Fraud Highest Yet

Hose Pipe Ban As South Coast Sizzles
Greedy Bosses Ask For More
Embryo Vote: Churchman Blasts Forth
'We're Not Christian Any More'.

Newly Weds 'Try Trampolining
If Your Love Life's Lacking Bounce'
AIDS Could Wipe Out 50 Million
Brave Brit Set For Title Pounce

death and wars condensed to headlines,
are we heading for the end?
bombs are loaded, but the news is:
Gazza Splits With His Girlfriend

INCUBATOR

In here
it is parched and desolate;
the warm wetness,
that which I rolled in
and made my shape,
has been taken

Now I lie
in dry light
and loud emptiness,
a harshclean drought
of pain;
no soft, deep dome
for me to curl into
and sleep

I am on a rack
of
wires and dials

Where is that which was me?
The moist
the my valley
in which I became

I have begun to fear

17

cHILD pRODIGY

i go to a special needs school
does that mean that im special
im just after nine and like making dinosaurs
i use words which are called swearing
it makes the teachers cross.
its my way of getting my own back
funny that isnt it
my own back
do you have your own back
i do

look

see its at the front now
when i swear
im saying something else inside
teachers notice me when i swear
it makes the others in our class laugh
my fathers girlfriend is having a baby
i hope its a girl
cos he doesnt like boys
i wonder if shell be like me
special

18

AN AFTERNOON AT THE
BOWLING GREEN

It was a lousy way to go.
Gurgling there on the suede grass verge
as the shirt-sleeved sun seared
behind parasol clouds.
Wherever it was you were going
it was nowhere near here.
Somebody's teacup fainted
and lay with you,
both askew,
not in their right place.
It was a low, English death.
Benches – Parks and Gardens grim green,
luncheon meat sandwiches on plain white plates,
custard creams and open-toe sandals.
Nearby a dog sat still as a doorstop,
placatory, needing comfort,
and when the ambulance came
you were virtually quiet
with an occasional shallow sigh
into the deep canyon oxygen mask.
There we were separated.
I was taken home,
went into the garden
and kicked the soil
you had hoed into powder
hoping to find you underneath it
still breathing.

MEMORY LAPSE

I cannot remember your eyes
What colour were they?
Brown, hazel, grey?
I cannot remember your eyes.

I cannot remember your chest
Did it have much hair?
Thick, dark or fair?
I cannot remember your chest.

I cannot remember your thoughts
How long did they last?
What were your last?
I cannot remember your thoughts.

I still can remember your back
A dark shrapnel patch
with nightmares to match
I still can remember your back.

SMALL WORLD

Consider the lilies
as you would sparrows
or frail empires,
so temporary;
yet recorded somewhere
a petal
a feather
a throne
so temporary

CONTRASTS

In the Holy of Holies
you hovered;
in the sweet lungs of your temple
you dreamed, composed and sang love songs
for clouds and condors to glide to.
Swam the olive oceans you did
where manta rays and starfish bloomed
as they fathomed out your shapes
in the swaying depths.

Now they cannot follow
as numb and naked you are,
heaped on to the gagging, garbage dump of our crimes,
our dark piles of pride
and gossiping pestilence.

Strange your journey
from the streaked skyscape of dawn's dyes
to this death;
koshered, limp lamb,
tender flesh
as flies paddle through the bloodstorm of your brow

To this bleak skip
we bring our borrowed breath
and take Yours
not stopped or shallow
but deeper and longer than time.

PLAYING AWAY

A Liverpudlian in Surrey explains Anfield
after Hillsborough

Often at night I hear voices
pub-loud,
exaggerating their way home
their phrasing and slow jokes
are a reminder
that I do not belong
here in these right-to-buy burrows
this motorway walled city.
Where I should be now
is beside the cellophane sea
with the awkward sentiments
inflammable mascots,
mis-spelt messages,
all the floating grief of my tribe.
We do not know
where to take our frenzy
apart from here.
We understand this place
this tip-up seat tabernacle
this turfed chalice.
It gives us hope,
for that is how we are.
We are not English,
our pain will not be neat,
nor our humanity dumb;
it will groan with flowers and fury.

THE CRYING GAME

Crying at airports when loved ones come home
Tears of relief that you're not left alone
Watching a soap, letting out a loud bawl
When the star in a coma doesn't die after all

Sniffling at weddings as love walks the aisle
And joy like confetti covers all in a smile
Christmas morn blubbing when you're given a pet
Sobbing at Wembley when your team finds the net

Weeping with laughter at a video clip
When a showing-off father loses his grip
Makes a bum-first-splash-landing, one of life's sports
A tarzan, whose rope broke, in pot-bellied shorts

Where do tears come from, some underskin vault?
These flash floods of feelings we can't seem to halt
These wordless expressions that leak down our cheek
Perhaps it's the heart longing to speak.

SONGS OF PRAISE

It is time to gather together
as we push our way through the swing doors,
and communicate group pattern greetings
from behind our dense, bonhomie gauze.

Gregarious fellowship follows
where the vocal urge all to join in,
and instruct us to cull inhibitions
by mis-naming shyness as sin.

Then as we assembled get frisky
and we're hugged by those whom we don't know,
whilst the room starts to throb like a mantra
we're concocting excuses to go.

Excessive behaviour in public
exhibits a rapturous tone,
as away in the stumbling darkness
preys the noiseless despair of alone.

For this is no place for a dreamer
as the boisterous cavort round the floor.
If joy is proclaimed through a megaphone
then I'm very unsure of the sure.

A souse has lost most powers of judgement
A disciple assumes that he's whole
Hard drinking will ruin your liver
but religion that shouts, drowns your soul.

HIGH WIRE ACT

If you're a high wire act
the view can be spectacular
especially when working in the open air,
crossing waterfalls and valleys,
that sort of thing.
However, winds can be a problem
as are hangovers and sneezing fits.

Yet, if you're a high wire act
people expect something more daring
than a ponderous glide
with a steadying pole.
They demand blindfolded leaps
from a wobbling unicycle
with no net
and a slithering pit
of adders far below.
And if you fall, they say
'Told you so. You were mad for trying it
in the first place'.

But if you're a high wire act
you get to see the sky
from the inside,
though when trying to explain
what it looked like
you are derided for being too fanciful
and thus not very useful.
But because you were so close
you actually heard the stars
and for a moment
your balance was perfect.

LIGHT RELIEF AT THE CIRCUS

Only been to the circus once
and that was in Sicily.
I, too, had the same dark jokes
about the clowns being funny,
or else.
Lions apologising to the Ring Master
for being too loud.
The gold filling trapeze artist
who chewed matches
and dropped those members of his troupe
who were behind with their payments.
Acrobats springing through the audience
lifting wallets and handbags,
a gaudy mêlée
of menace and claustrophobia.
But it wasn't like that at all.
We had the best seats in the house
which belonged to two people
who had failed to turn up
for some reason or other.

ABOVE HEATHROW AT NIGHT
A DRIFTING ANGEL CONSIDERS
THE EARTH

This is an immense evening
one for the observant and the sensate
Initially I will say
'Over there is Shepperton, or Staines
or Windsor'
a guessed-at A–Z of yellow suburbs
But if the image is painted
what I see is
a slug's trail of halogen heading for Oxford,
neon varicose veins
meandering away from the M4 artery,
forked lightning trunk roads
clotted with diamanté roundabouts,
mucous motorways.

And further north
a gold-braided kippa of street lights
over Hendon and Golders Green.
And then I will wonder
where all this is leading;
perhaps to a heart somewhere
a breathing foundation
a centre from which you journey

As I now fly off
to hover above other planets
to see where they are going.

A MORNING'S WORK

*During the Gulf conflict, advertisers frantically outbid
one another to secure prime-time slots during main news
programmes on Independent Television*

Jason is making a phone call
from his desk in SW3
a policeman outside clamps a Volvo
and there's not a leaf left on the tree.

Jason is doing the business
as tanks trawl across desert sands
winter winds swirl a McDonald's bag
whilst Sloane Street is blowing its hands.

Jason is pleased with the outcome
round the block a thief tries a car door
a product that was in the doldrums
now revived by a faraway war.

Jason is having a coffee
shells like a plague swarm about
on Knightsbridge the traffic is dreadful
as napkins and cloths are smoothed out.

Jason is booking a table
at a place just off Brompton Road
where nearby without coded warning
a litter bin waits to explode.

0898

So sorry not to phone
I had to mow the lawn
the kids have wrecked the grass
it's looking dry and worn
And then there was the car
it made this awful sound
I had to take it in
it cost me ninety pound
But now we're quite alone
everybody's out
I like it when you talk
with that cutie pout
You're just a call away
heard but never seen
and it's completely safe
having sex with a machine.

WORKING MOTHER

I catch the early shoppers' train
leaves Leeds at half past eight
with women who are Harrods bound
from headscarved Harrogate
I change my clothes at King's Cross
from bland to vivid bait
I'm a working mother
earning jam for tea

In a hotel called The Harlequin
with carpets that are bald
I offer several services
at least that's what they're called
But there's no real variation
in a fifteen minute maul
I'm a working mother
hoping to get home

My husband, Lenny, drove an HGV
through France and Spain
He'd always add three extra days
so he could see Elaine
He was all the while in Pontefract
no more postcards from the Seine
I'm a working mother
going home for tea

Lenny lives in Dewsbury now
Elaine's in Tenerife
with a nightclub act called Ricci Rome
whose real name is Keith

They own a bungalow called 'My Way'
in hedge-clipped Haywards Heath
Elaine, the sequinned mother,
she's not working

My Alice is a princess
likes puppies, dolls and pink
Wayne, he's three years older
wants his own ice skating rink
One day they'll know
by which time I'll be dead from drink
They're my babies
they need an earning mother

Please don't tell them
that I'm a working mother.

A DISAPPOINTING RECITAL

Try as I might
I cannot make the sound of birds
though I have been in this cage
for years
It is not a deliberate reluctance
more a fear
of how I sound to others.

I have attempted several songs,
spent long hours perfecting them,
practised in front of the mirror,
described them as arias
in imaginary interviews
But when a small crowd gathered
to hear these works
what came out was something else.

Since then
I have become a connoisseur of silences
an explorer of the unsaid
Yet I still know
what these melodies sound like in my soul
and hope one day
they will be properly expressed.

I BELIEVE

I believe in one God, the Father Almighty
Although I have problems with the word Father,
what happens if he was violent, drunk, or just not there?
Maker of Heaven and Earth
and of things visible and invisible
which is a bit of a puzzle
because if something exists but is invisible
how do you know when it isn't there?
And in one Lord Jesus Christ
I believe Jesus was a great cook.
Oh to be given a fish prepared by Him.
I believe in imagination.
Imagine no imagination,
hard to imagine.
God of God
Light of Light
By Whom all things were made
Who for us men, and for our salvation
came down from Heaven;
presumably that means women as well.
I believe in women.
So does the Church of Scotland,
but that's possibly to spite the English General Synod.
The Anglicans two thirds believe in women
providing they can set up a Working Party
to discuss having a conference
at the end of which a Report is issued
confirming the matter is under consideration
depending on the vote
seventeen years later.
Methodists and Baptists acknowledge women
but not so as you'd notice

Brethren and Pentecostals are constantly surprised
to discover that such an object as a woman exists.
But Charismatics fully accept women –
providing they can edify the worship
with lots of swirly dancing,
and don't wobble unnecessarily.
I believe that if I believed in reincarnation
I would come back as anything but a woman
a cowpat
or an escalator perhaps
at least with both those categories
you don't stay trodden on for very long.
I believe in women
I believe in women
I believe in women
but leadership is male
leadership is stale
leadership is frail.
I believe leaders should be servants
and servants should be powerless.
I believe all leaders should spend part of their training
playing on merry-go-rounds and building sandcastles
I believe the church should be a refuge, a swing park,
an embrace.
I believe that at the beginning of the next
International Healing Crusade
at some conference hall cathedral
the platform party should begin worship
by doing farmyard impressions
followed by a competition
to find the best yodeller.
I believe in absurdity
such as kangaroos,
cockatoos,
and saying the word 'bobble'.

I believe that people
who, in deep sincerity, go forward for healing
and do not experience it
and are then told by the leader
it is because of their lack of faith
should then be able to belt that leader,
and then minister to him about his sin
of using emotional blackmail
as a means of control in public meetings.
I believe in the gifts of the Spirit;
bullying sick people isn't one of them.
I believe in the supernatural, mysticism,
and the raising of the dead;
it's just that there's not much call for it
at our mid-week prayer meeting.
I have problems with people who proclaim
that there's a man at the back suffering with lumbago,
when in fact it's a woman in the gallery, with cystitis.
It all seems so confusing,
so speculative.
For that reason
I don't play one-armed bandits either.
Not that I have problems with gambling,
after all, what are investments
but balance-sheet bets, FT tick-tack?
The revenue from these little flutters
has kept some Christian organisations going for years.
I believe Prosperity Teaching is a rabbit's foot
being waved at the reality of poverty.
I believe we need a theology of money.
I believe in confession –
not positive, or negative – just confession.
I believe in what my friend Martin said:
'drama is a tool, but theatre is art'.
I believe propaganda is ideological Valium.

Propagandists are mynah birds,
excellent mimics,
but don't expect them to say anything original.
I believe in doubt
I believe doubt is a process of saying
'Excuse me, I have a question'.
Propagandists hate questions
and in so doing
detest art,
I believe in art.
I acknowledge one baptism
for the remission of sins.
I believe we should seek the lost, unhealed child
in all of us,
cradle it, and say,
'you really are forgiven'.
And I look for the resurrection of the dead.
No more hearses
or death's graveside curses,
and the life of the world to come.
I believe
I believe in quite a lot.

IN THE HOLLOW POOLS OF EVENING TENNYSON IS HERE AGAIN

In the hollow pools of evening
I search for your mystery
As the sea soaks up the shingle
Gulls wade through your Deity

I strayed to the coast that glistens
Sang its oil-silt lullaby
Waves, I beg thee, pure this spillage
Lest I stiffen from the dye

Where's the Anchor on the foreshore?
Or the nails in drifts of wood?
Will the undercurrents claim me?
Has the Life Guard gone for good?

Lazarus, still as a pecked crab
Bound in seaweed when he died
Washed up from the brine of passing
On to Heaven's rising tide

All this loneliness may sour me
One wing bird attempting flight
If there is a dune of healing
May I nest where there is light

BEACH

Sand,
the coast's grained, brown ribs
beckon the whisked blood of the ocean,
the transfusion begins
and the pebbles cheer the union.

Through small pyramids and plains of shells
a curlew excavates,
whilst lug worms,
like underground weavers,
leave threads of mud
on the sewn surface of the linen beach.

Gulls mewl,
a swoop of bitter babies
searching for nature's eternal milk,
and the sky frowns
like a bloodhound
wondering where to look next.

Out at sea,
a boat; its movement
imperceptible from here;
and my breaths, like the clouds,
have been indexed
to the last tide.

And the breeze belts about
like a flamenco dancer
with no set steps,
but it sounds ordered
and in its own harmony.

CAMUS-NA-CROISE

Apart from shorn sheep smears of cloud
the sky is Wild West blue.
Scooped pools on the tidal shore
contain aquatic plantations
of swaying copses
and thin spin life.
Seaweed trees lean green
to the current
as crabs,
beneath dry toast domes,
dash and dawdle through their days,
sideways,
on their buckled legs.
Fish, smaller than raindrops, are stationary
then flit as if flicked
by invisible fingers.
Nearby, gulls,
plaster of Paris white,
course wheeling climbs
to scheme their removal.
Meanwhile,
a seahorse,
more vivid than harebells,
rears and canters
through the rippling valley.

For Maisie May

THE LAST WASP SINGS

The last wasp sings
before falling in autumn,
still distinguishable,
above the bronze battlefield
of once airborne leaves.
Wind and age are the culprits
for this beautiful death.

The last wasp sings
of a meadow now in coma,
a villa of nature in which
flowers bubbled with pollen
in the warm womb
of its summer earth.

The last wasp sings
before entering twilight,
a dark girdle wrapped
around its buttercup back.
The last wasp sings
of a palette which daubed it,
and on a final low flight
it gleams towards
a brilliant end.

DOWN HERE, UP THERE

Down here – we've got peace treaties with guns
down here – we've got luke warm hot-cross buns
down here – we've got Porsches, pearls and slums
a mishmash of massed mortals mope down here

Down here – we wear tinsel, tat and tweed
down here – we say creeds we'll never need
down here – we've got Bill and Ben and Little Weed
the jumble sale called life is what's down here

Up there – there are trees and flowers that fly
up there – gorillas stroll the sky
up there – is the dolphin's liquid cry
starfish ceilidh daily way up there

Up there – there's a sapphire sun at dawn
up there – countless clouds of never born
up there – ride the Golden Unicorn
the child that never was is named up there

Down here – we've got royals on camera three
down here – chattering to Sue Lawley
down here – you'll hear rhymes which are dodgy
passing things amuse us d-d-down here

Down here – we get yearnings for the past
down here – we take lovers who don't last
down here – there's a huge supporting cast
sound bites and soap operas star down here

Up there – there are colours you don't know
up there – is a planet made of snow
up there – there is no such thing as 'No'
You can skateboard down a rainbow when you're there

Up there – the angels move in shoals
up there – meet the martyrs full of holes
up there – there's no apartheid of the soul
touch the power and the glory when you're there
it's the healing old, old story read up there
the lamb, the lion and scapegoat reign up there.

ONLY AT EASTER

Whips circled and crudely landed
to lash life out of Him,
or so it appeared.
Spikes were summoned
to close the stone vault,
and the sky growled.
Haughty robes of passing power
flapped through women wailing,
towards, unknowingly, the chasm of pride,
the withered well of no comfort.
How much those perished priests,
like us,
didn't know.

Rising, He rose.
Risen, He remains.
His remains, apart from some ruby drops,
He took with Him.
They became our passport out of death,
our living ascent from a
lifeless climate.
His scent of wounds,
in which we are now wrapped,
carried us out of that petrified place
into the calm city
where even the dust has been healed.

WINOS

Garbled they gather
for slurred pow-wows.
A ragged wreath of
blown bubble-gum eye-lids,
and facial scabs
collected through slumping.

Where do they come from
these snoring sky divers
now sprawled at our feet?
They must have fallen from somewhere.

Where pigeons smother city squares,
that is their saloon,
a cocktail hour that lasts for days
on a cackling afternoon.

Even when sober they stagger,
their shaking systems in a rage with them
as their twitching limbs
try sneaking away unpunished.
Off for another encore of paralytic opera
a howling libretto
sung for the sake of the soloist.

It has been suggested by other tyrannies
we regard them as slops,
swaying swill congealed into human forms
maintained by lighter fuel and warm air ducts.
They are the image we avoid

They are a void image
and could not have been made in anyone's image
and nobody will miss them.
Some governments achieve popularity this way.

FUTURE SHOCK

Where does this thick silence come from
with banishment of words?
Has someone swift with chloroform
smothered all the birds?

Will it stay songless at morning?
No Universe deep tone
Need we, too, burn for purity
A renitent St Joan?

Yet is this quietness preferable
to that which will commence
when God, the groom of chastity,
vaults the Astral fence

With canticles of rushing Truth
composed by stellar light?
Will He not find a blemished bride
and mournful wedding night?

How to atone for such whoredom?
What will our sentence be?
Here is our foretaste of exile,
this soundless purgatory.

TOUGH LOVE

Yours is a tough love
You ask us to come to You
and then put us on
blitzed housing estates
where slime walls sweat green
and some of the inhabitants
have bombed themselves
before the One O'clock News.
Yours is a tough love
You abandon us in
fluorescent de-tox units
where the mad dream loudly;
and, by the way,
whatever happened to Monica Coughlan
and all those other Mary Magdalenes
whose riches are thirty quid
and a damp mattress?

                    Mine is no off-the-cuff love
                    I stand before the powerful,
                    the plausible, the negligent,
                    and make note of their policies.
                    There will be a reckoning.
                    Have you not listened to
                    My shaking sobs for those who
                    erase themselves?
                    My grief makes mountains cower
                    It seems My distress
                    may have deafened you.

But Yours is a rough love
which apparently walks past
the cardboard caves
where there is only space
for the blank
and the bereaved.
And Yours is a rough love
that leaves us here
in this raging plague of need
with our earnest intentions
and widow's mite resources

Mine is no bluff love
for I've been
where you'll never go,
even beyond
the end of breath
to gather in
the addled
and the disappointed.
Mine is enough love
to brace you
through the Bedlam
of My soiled
and spoiled images.
So weep
and turn over tables with Me
I have heard your heart
and Mine
is
enough love

I HAD TO CREATE

I had to create
I could not but make and shape
I started with silence
the amoeba of inspiration
and began before the beginning.
When you think of Me
you imagine the Universe
to you it is limitless,
worthy of respect and seminars
academic symposiums
equations on paper.
Let Me help you.
Limitless is a finite word.
Limitless is merely My fingernail.
Am I overwhelming you?
I hope so.
When ideas take shape there are sounds
and so it proved to be.
And after that
I dreamt Myself, in miniature.
From Me came him
From him came her
Out of Me both you became
My working sculptures
My holy union
My rapturous endeavour.
When you then touched
did you not tingle and feel Me?
Was it not eros undefiled
without guilt?

I brought Myself from everywhere
in order that you might be.
There you were, My darling pair,
decorated by light
fed from seeds
nourished by the elements
given rhythm by seasons
and voices that sang of stars and seahorses.
But know,
that to you only
I gave the rudder of this place
holding My heart incarnate
the root of you.
While all around you
the cell and sinew of My understanding.
When a lioness stares
and then rolls over
I know what she's saying.
When chimpanzees embrace,
then race
screaming through branches . . .
When
When
When
When . . .

WHEN THERE WAS NOTHING

When there was nothing
There was I
Lighting volcanoes
Stretching the sky
Sketching the veins of an acorn leaf
Painting the gloss on the tiger's teeth

When there was nothing
I was there
Buffing the buffalo
Grooming the bear
Curling the cobra in his coiled-up cave
Rippling the river and frothing the wave

When there was nothing
There was Me
Expanding the girth
of the Redwood tree
Moulding the moon whilst counting the bugs
And no matter if you're squeamish
But I even made the slug

When there was nothing
Just I AM
Before I'd even offered you
My punctured lamb
I juggled all the planets
Then equipped the frog
With the energetic means
To leap from log to bog

When there was nothing
There was I
When there was nothing
I was there
When there was nothing
There were always Three
Spirit
Son
        and Me.

WHOSE EARTH?

It took six days to complete and then two thousand
  years to wreck
When you're on it it's enormous,
Viewed from space a blue-white speck –
A marble in the darkness, an ornament of peace
But we're the drunken landlord that's now tearing up
  the lease

> Whose Earth?
> God's Earth
> Nicotine turf
> How to get it clean?

We've been into laboratories and messed around with
  things,
invented bombs, the compact disc, Semtex and onion
  rings
Created swamps of effluence, then get into our cars
as our exhausts like rapiers inflict dioxide scars

> Whose Earth?
> God's Earth
> Nicotine turf
> How to get it clean?

Black bird in Arabia who started out so white
glued fast to tarmac beaches on a day which looks like
  night,
its clogged-up gullet closing jerks the air for frenzied
  sips

whilst the sky is raining particles which shouldn't touch
  our lips

                    Whose Earth?
                    God's Earth
                    Nicotine turf
                    How to get it clean?

Yet this is still a garden great with growth and many
  moods
From the mists of Ardnamurchan where the golden
  eagle broods
to the deep trees of the Amazon and the hot heart of
  Sudan
God surveys the disrepair and the steward of it, man.

                    Whose Earth?
                    God's Earth
                    Nicotine turf
                    How to get it clean?

SOAP OPERA

I'm a soap opera substitute human
I never go out of the house
After years of continuous Brookside
I'm completely word perfect in Scouse

I'm a soap opera substitute human
A Home and Away avid fan
dragging my fantasy surfboard
in search of a fantastic tan

I'm a soap opera substitute human
A Rover's Return drinking type
feeding my prize winning pigeons
with plates of inedible tripe

I'm a soap opera substitute human
A non-U EastEnder who smokes
Doing deals which involve dodgy motors
a spiv sipping dark rum and Cokes

I'm a soap opera substitute human
Taking The High Road to hope
whilst sounding my heart with Young Doctors
via a script writer's stethoscope

I'm a soap opera substitute human
a bereft Ramsay Street refugee
familiar with all the inhabitants
but not one of the Neighbours knows me.

THIS IS WHERE I AM

This is where I am
always now, arms outstretched
free moving
no longer riveted to my wooden crypt.
Like a sparrow, I am everywhere;
running recklessly through Belfast's sobbing streets
and Soweto's furious evenings
I comfort and bathe the slashed and snapped,
the last thing some soldiers hear
is Me grieving over them.

In all your repetitive quarrels and polite slander,
your tug of war negotiations
in the Valium aftermath of a slammed door,
Mine is the voice that says 'Come closer,
it doesn't have to be like this'.
This is where I am
in the precinct
in the prison
in the lonely maisonette
in the desert of your little days
This is where I am
offering heart transplants
to the wounded and the weary,
teaching the stiff and graceless
how to embrace.

ON HEARING GOOD NEWS

On hearing good news what to do?
To sneak up on ghosts and go 'boo!'
Or swim the Atlantic,
an interesting antic,
providing there isn't a queue.

I'd go and get drunk if I drank
or plan some spectacular prank.
Then I'd buy a guitar
from a backward bazaar
and call myself Marvin B. Hank.

I'd swallow twelve oysters as well
removing them first from their shell.
And I'd hire chorus girls
to do-wop 'String of Pearls'
and hope that my breath doesn't smell.

On hearing good news I'd go daft
toss a coin up and down like George Raft.
He wore a trilby
which rhymes with Kim Philby,
Now I wonder if he ever laughed?

I'd stealthily climb up a tree
as heights do not much bother me
I'd find a large squirrel
and christen him Cyril,
that's the name of a former MP.

On hearing good news I'd be cowed
for I'm a quiet vicar from Stroud
I'm nothing it seems
with nonsensical dreams
I'll just sing the next hymn very loud.

THE UNICORN IN THE ABATTOIR

Through the open double doors
the unicorn was dragged
into the white tiled chamber
with its bevelled blood gully
This meek beast
had once hurdled the clouds;
but for lingering too long
the meat traders got him,
the raw glistening gouges
on his haunches
confirming their fingerprints
about his cream torso.

Now he slipped and slithered
across the callous cobbles
towards the stun-man's splattered apron,
his pearl hooves
too pure for the earth's coarse paths
his mane virtually no more.

For if something is too beautiful
one of us will deface it, rip it out.
His golden horn
also hacked off
leaving a fist of gristle,
myrrh seeping from its jagged stump.

Later, when it came to carving him up
no blade was sharp enough
to sever the limbs
So he was thrown

whole
on to the fire outside
where he still burns
attracting those with a scent of balm
and the need for warmth.

I DON'T LIKE MEN

I don't like men
they're loud and rather coarse
they have a funny smell
I much prefer a horse

I don't like men
they think they're always right
that's such a weight to bear
when they're really not that bright

I don't like men
they leave me rather numb
A consequence of meeting
the emotionally dumb

I don't like men
yet when I air this view
some women shout me down
I wonder why they do?

I don't like men
my maiden's bubble burst
I can't lie down and love
as my daddy got there first

I don't like men
It's better with Yvonne
It's probably my fault
I must have led him on.

HOW TO SPEAK LOVE IN A STORM?

How to speak love in a storm?
depends on the substance of the voice
as the trees rage
and roof tiles smash,
where seagulls are grounded
and there is only chaos.

How to speak love in a storm?
is to put up a signpost for the lost
as on the bitter hillside
you lie, murmuring
'Why is this happening now?'
Exposure, like a fox,
circling your lamb's heart.

How to speak love in a storm?
means finding the right inflection
Not offering words and hollow prayers
but walking backwards with you
into your abandoned years.

QUEST

When you are healed
it will be that you are ready
The locked basement
full of sobbing
having been finally heard

For down there
are toys,
handbags for dressing up with,
and unexplained visitors
to corrupt you into silence

When you grew up
you learned a different vocabulary
it was in your interest to do so
it was expected.
Yet now
you even sneeze like a child.

YOU DO NOT SLEEP OLD

You do not sleep old as you imagine
numb as a lead-shot sparrow,
or fade fallow
soil crumbled by monotonous churning
dry of all blood
waiting for the slow-step wind
to be your pall bearer

For these are your shooting bloom years
deep lapping acres of unexpected buds and harvests
and although inside you now
death offers its dark jewels
beneath a coarse canopy of thunder
soon this trading will cease
the roar will be sealed
within its own muffled mausoleum

And you will make the sound of swallows and heather
hearing again the song
that only your soul knows.

COMPASSION: THE SMALL PRINT

Compassion lies down with the wasting
as scorpions of death quick-step past,
where a legion of underfed icons
take part in a withering fast.

Compassion turns over tables
and then tends to go for the throat
of those whose riches are suspect,
for Compassion has only one coat.

Compassion was flayed without mercy
abused on a tree's bitter bark.
The grim sky left widowed and shaking
as God wept alone in the dark.

Compassion considers our values.
Our occasional thoughts of the stripped
whilst we turn to the share-index tables
to check if our profits have dipped.

Compassion cleaves fast to the leaking.
Those holy reflections, like us.
For there in the midst of the maelstrom
Jesus is cleaning their pus.

Compassion is waiting with patience
to see if our hearts can discern
our heat in the fire of the Gospel.
To smoke, or to recklessly burn.

SEARCH PARTY

The world is changing quickly
and it makes me feel quite sickly
and now success is based on what I earn.
The weather's getting hotter
and just like a drunken potter
I'm really not sure which way I should turn.

I was going to be a Goth
I was going to be Frank Bough
I even went to church with tidy hair
but a new opinion poll expressed indifference to the soul
with just a vague belief that something broods out there.

So I bought some gourmet books
written by accomplished cooks
full of recipes from North, South, West and East
but I lost my appetite
when the poor came into sight
led by Jesus, famished Saviour of the least.

Now you may think me rather barmy
off I went to join the army
but it doesn't seem to be there anymore.
For there's a changing, new world order
but if you dare cross my border
we've still weapons for a 20-minute war.

So should I put my trust in money?
Be a health freak like Bugs Bunny,
or maybe heavy metal is the way?

But what remains a mystery
is 2000 years of history
doesn't seem to have worked out a better way.

I'm really not sure which way I should turn.
We've still weapons for a 20-minute war.
Led by Jesus, famished Saviour of the least.
A vague belief that something broods out there.
Doesn't seem to have worked out a better way
a better way
a better way.

DIPLOMATIC SOLUTION

We didn't all climb in the wagons
and go quietly off to the camps.
Raise your hands, fellow seekers for justice,
if you've ever been turned into lamps.

What kind of agenda's been drafted
as you sit and discuss who we are?
When we come to the Conference Table
must we still wear a yellow star?

You visit our ghetto and judge us
demanding an orchard of peace,
back home you do things with electrodes
you omit from your oiled press release.

You lord it like some feudal baron
endlessly gorging on quail.
For your peasants, a grand, legal process,
where the innocent end up in jail.

And now your contempt seems so pious
as you highlight our barbaric acts,
whilst concealed in your chambers of Statehood
your dissenters are trussed up in sacks.

Moses concealed a dead body,
God's chosen were forced on the run.
David had lust as his counsel,
nothing's new under the sun.

We're all selling arms to each other.
Each one as guilty as hell.
So why is it when you go public,
you have such a sanctified smell?

STATEMENT OF FAITH

I'm soft on hell
and mushy on sin.
How can a soul be lost
if it's not playing to win?

I'm wishy on grace
and washy on prayer.
I'll be starting my fast
after this last éclair.

I'm spongy on tongues
But not bad on hope.
Have I gone multi-faith
for admiring the Pope?

I'm weak on the bible
and remembering things.
How long was St Paul
one of Israel's kings?

One thing is sure
I'll lie under the sod
And let my headstone say
'He was quite keen on God'.

THE UNFASHIONABLE NOTES OF RABBI KLEIN

(i)   You send me a Christmas card
        with a derivative greeting
        'Dear Shylock,
        so you bleed.
        So?'

(ii)   I have considered my position
        in the light of your negotiations.
        I get to lie down in lime pits
        bit by bit.
        Right?

(iii)   Ah yes. The conspiracy.
        The media, the banks, the future
        where all will eat bagels.
        So what's wrong with bagels?
        Only joking.
        (Crack a gag before they crack you)

(iv)   Of course we fear the Judgement
        but then we have some good lawyers.
        It's going to be a long argument
        There are some things too deep in us
        to be cross examined

(v)   Esther, how we needed you
        in Warsaw, in York, in Berlin,
        all those other tombs.
        Where were you?

(vi)   If we get to embrace God
         then it must be in private,
         wedding nights are not for public viewing.

(vii)   So maybe on that day
         God will say to us
         'Sing anything, but please not "Shalom Aleichem".
         Oy, oy, oy . . . that song'.
         Maybe not. Just another joke.

AN OXBRIDGE TUTOR CONSIDERS THE COMING ACADEMIC YEAR

A new intake of spiral curls
slinks through the cashpoint streets
whilst chaps with brogues and floppy hair
dream of nocturnal treats

And I will speak complexities
of Sartre's fish-eyed ways
while contemplating towpath love
in last year's lapping haze

For I was only temporary
in her syllabus of fire
that soon went out and left instead
a charred and bitter spire

So I take another Rennies
yet several laps from death
I slowly rise where once I sprang
a panther short of breath.

SPLITTING HEADACHE

I hung upside down from my parachute
Far above, the instructor told lies
As I hurtled through flocks of Canadian geese
Down below, such impending surpri . . .

SEASIDE FRANKENSTEIN:
McGONAGLE'S BRAIN IN
BETJEMAN'S HEART

Skegness, O Skegness
you're not up to much
After the Ice Age the North Sea it melted
which is why you are British not Dutch

Torquay, sweet Torquay
with your palm trees and hot dogs
And sometimes tourists bump into each other
because of the sea fogs

Lowestoft, stark Lowestoft
amongst your shingle I forage
But now the East Wind is flapping my trousers
so I'll head back to Norwich

Blackpool, grand Blackpool
with your miles and miles of sands
It's also Europe's most polluted beach
which is why I have swollen glands

Minehead, quaint Minehead
Somerset's finest
Bracing breezes which help cure the bronchial trouble
and also those who have sinus

Lyme Regis, Lyme Regis
with cafés which serve carrots and mince
Years ago Meryl Streep made a film there
and she hasn't been back since.

FOR WHEN OUR HEARTS WEEP GLORIOUS

For when our hearts weep glorious
relieved of all this miserable
roll down canyons careless we
echoing with glee and goodness
forming visions in the scampering dust
and skimming frisbees made of sunspots

For when our hearts weep glorious
weightless of all bitter slump
sparkling as a beach we all
then burrow through the sighing waves
to play see-saw with driftwood and shells

For when our hearts weep glorious
for when our hearts shout what a hoot
for when our hearts skip round and round
for when our hearts beat lots and more
then there we race in radiance
and all those dreams are then and now
and after that there is no fade
For when our hearts swoop without fall
outshines all
the one who paid

MAY IT BE . . .

May it be a place of learning
but not a bit like school
may angels be angelic here
telling jokes and playing pool
May it fondle folk in places
where they've never felt before
embrace the up and downright
especially the whore
May it pad with Christ the tiger
through the jungles of our fears
be the first at whispered funerals
with the ministry of tears
May it rage at legislation
that makes God weep in the night
may it glide above the drunken streets
swoop down with wings of light
May it storm into the boardroom
and implore: 'you must repent'
may it spurn smooth economics
and pay the widow's rent
May it put on plays that puzzle
and dances for the lame
may it pirouette when fast asleep
may it stoke the holy flame
May it be a place of silence
for those who've lost their voice
may it bore down on the boring
with a cry of 'now rejoice'
may it be . . . may it be . . .
may it be . . . may it be . . .

TRAVELS

DUSK AND ICONS

The sky is a dappled dove fresco
buffed pale and failing,
as Rome rambles round itself towards evening.
In chipped chapels
under gold-leaf heavens
saints plead in an incense twilight
and Madonnas soothe their stone sucklings.

On the rubbed rust piazzas
churches constantly cross themselves,
as inside,
wakes of burning batons
cremate the silence
with their flickering music
mourning Christ the wilted.

Marble statues and orphan columns
glide across bridges
on their stone tightropes.
The slipping sun has bounced down the clouds
just missing the suburbs' rouge roofs.
On domes, above arches,
angels beyond census
see no night.

PISA TO FLORENCE

And I saw a thousand sunflowers
applauding themselves
to be joined by more,
these glowing orbs of numerous summers
host to a carnival of bees.

The sun hung ripe
on that humming morning
as God laughed
beyond these blooms of His imagination.
It must have been
a practical plantation
supporting factories
the food chain
bureaucratic mountains
and accountants.

But for just then
it was the earth getting its own back
before this crowd of Van Gogh's comforters
began to buckle
nodding towards the soil
cascading their perpetual seed
eluding the clinical scythe.

AT THE EDGE OF AMERICA

Three pelicans,
the colour of evening smoke
flap and flow
barely above the cream waves.
It is as if
they are icing
the end of the ocean
to then rise and plunge
through the Atlantic's foamed fancy.

On the plump shore
a ladybird is grunting up
shelves of sand.
Soon she is crossing
the vast plateau of a footprint.
She is a lacquered dodgem,
fraught and sun-spotted,
in search of a flat, cool planet.
Below,
her pitted route is
tyre-tracked
tightly packed
pecking at her ballet-blocked feet.

Up the blurred coast
Ocean City is a corrugated mirage.
Tonight,
after the haze,
the Metropolis will again wear
too many luminous trinkets.

Meanwhile,
here
the ocean has so many songs
and not one have we heard before.

MEAGRE GLORY

By the huddled fires of hardship,
as the night-wind peels the sand.
Blankets curve round bone-bag bodies
held in place by shrivelled hands.

Beneath the dunes snakes, like snipers,
creep and scheme through Nature's war.
In this vault of looted treasures,
a holy gem bleeds for the poor.

Here, where wild dogs hunt each other,
morse code threat of growl and bark.
Serrated insects creak their chorus
as the blaze shrinks back to dark.

Kneels a figure stained with grieving,
stroking heads with skewered palms.
Jesus, jewel of the ruined,
holds them in His wasted arms.

WISH YOU WERE HERE: BANGKOK

This is not what I made you for
as glitter on a strobe-strewn floor
a stop-off on a package tour
and I really want to take you Home tonight

Your life now filled with grunting men
who pay in dollars, deutschmark, yen
lust's quick routine disrobes again
and I really want to take you Home tonight

Your limbs were never meant for this
to strut near such a dark abyss
so please accept my holy kiss
and I really want to take you Home tonight

This is not what I made you for
but I can make an open door
and lead you out, as we implore
please let us take you Home tonight
you'll be safe if you come Home tonight

PLAYTHING

You should be playing with dolls
and teaching them how to sit straight
You should be playing with dolls
and tucking them in when it's late

You should be counting the clouds
and squelching the mud through your toes
You should be counting the clouds
and avoiding blowing your nose

You should be grazing your knee
By running through fields far too fast
You should be grazing your knee
and squealing at bugs that creep past

You should be flying a kite
and when it breaks, getting vexed,
You should be flying a kite
then asking: 'What to do next?'

You should be playing with dolls
my frail lamb of unblemished fleece
You should be playing with dolls
You should be sleeping in peace.

AND THESE ALL THESE

And these, all these are mine
I know each sinew of their small frames
I hear their fear of night
I watch their fun
and when they laugh, so do I
In joy I see them invent themselves
even their shyness is a delight to me
I cherish their innocence
And these, all these are mine.
And if, when I return,
I find just one who has been defiled
One desecrated by your corruption
One invaded by your lust
One chained to your perversion
One burgled of purity
One dominated by your tyranny
One diseased through your indulgence
One famished by your inequity
One reliant on your base favours
One separated from Me through your wicked fancy,
One, who once was Mine
Then I promise
You will never see the sun again
All you will receive is darkness
it will have no end
and you will not know peace
It will be terrible and just on that day
because these, all these are Mine.

LOST HORIZON

I live in a small, lonely land of chrome
clothes shops, building societies and
detached cardboard boxes with riverside
views and close to all amenities.

My country has long skies where crystal
birds raise their praising wings to the
furnace sun.

Where I live, ponds freeze over in
winter, cling-filmed by the skating night.
If our pipes burst, we telephone for a man
and my father grumbles.

Outside our hut spiders stalk flies like
spies on a dark mission. Sometimes when
the rains fall, so does our home. My
mother has weary eyes and buried babies.

I am nearly not a child but a demanding
consumer. I walk the cellophane
corridors of Toys R Us pointing and
picking toys that bounce and shoot; toys
that are decoys for an embrace, for a kiss.

I make things with twine and driftwood. I
imagine your cities and build them from
shells and stones. From watching you I
am beginning to learn envy and discontent.
I may not be a child for too long. In
Cambodia there are pits – shallow scoops
of earth where I will curl up and become
manure.

Nobody trains you to be a child, yet I am
being taught to compete, acquire, possess,
collect trinkets, that adults regard as
triumph. Somewhere in it all I want to be
a child.

In order to remain a child, I will need
several vaccinations, but when the creamy
moon floats in the mocha sky, I hear wild,
wise words that no one's told me. It says:
'If you are harmed, I have millstones . . . '

I, too, hear this soft tongue whispering
through Arndale's stringed arcades. It
says: 'This is a bad place for your
imagination – why not share Mine?' It
says: 'Your poverty is not apparent but I
will burn your braided rags.'

It says: 'I am your personal invitation.
Mention My Name at the door.'

PLAYGROUND

I'm in my playground here by the sea
where we race through the cooked sand my friends and me
and I've got this funny cough and it's called TB

My father's a fisherman and he goes out to sea
but it's best when he comes back and I climb onto his knee
and he pats my funny cough which is called TB

I've got a toy which my father made me
What's your name?   I'm called Marie
and I've got this funny cough, and it's called TB

MOURNING AFTER

If you die I will replace you with another
but it will not have your name
Why is it someone so new
crumbles quickly in these short hours
as life's maggots loot your fading breath
growing gross on what was yours?
Like a lioness, I will mate again
for you, my cub, are too weak to tumble
too withered to pounce
too frail to be inquisitive.
And who now hears my roars
from this hunched vault of inevitable grief?
And the gnawing night clings like a lizard
There was so much of you to celebrate
God of distance and comfort
let this sick shawl of hope
now leap into Your Presence.
If you die, I will replace you with another
but it will not have your name.

HOUSE-PROUD

He
This is my palace for you, my love,
No gold, no marble, just wood;
No seagull-white pillars or porticos
No shaved lawns outside – just mud.

She
This is my palace for you, my love,
A chair, a cupboard, a floor;
A table to polish and put things on,
A mansion of flowers, a door.

This is my palace for you, my love,
No armchairs, no toilet, just wood;
No wickerwork cot to put babies in,
No tap to turn on – no good.

This is my palace for you, my love,
A robe, a gala, a fleece;
Arms cradling us from the mire below,
An ark in the swill, a peace.

CATHEDRAL

You have built so many cathedrals
weaved arches of intricate praise
you have fashioned devotional chapels
where hymn books have seen better days

You have sharpened stone spires into needles
perhaps to point out that I reign
you have filled up the peace with your clutter
and frescos depicting my pain

You have tried to portray me as Gothic
Byzantine, Renaissance and Greek
you have made me the Lord of the mighty
but rarely a friend of the meek

So now, you will visit my Temple
of debris, infection and blight
Come join me and my crumpled servants
for this is a true, holy site.

RAPPED FISH

My toil has freed you
from the unsure bet
of trying to make it home
without a hole in your net
but should that aqua calamity
befall you
I know you can't swim
so this is what I will do
I'll walk across the waves again
locate the tear
because I am the needle
and you're the repair

And the octopus is capable
of hugging eight of you
he's a deep water fountain pen
who writes to me in blue
and the seahorse needs no reins
nor the dogfish a lead
but keep your toes out the water
when the shark's about to feed
and do not fear the night
for that's when I stroke the whales
and banter with the manta rays
and sharpen up their tails

My toil has freed you
from the unsure bet
of trying to make it home
without a hole in your net
but should that aqua calamity

befall you
I know you can't swim
so this is what I will do
I'll walk across the waves again
locate the tear
because I am the needle
and you're the repair
I said I am the needle
and you're the repair

ON BEING A PIG

I am, as you see, a pig,
a pink bubble of refuse.
Some of us are brown, pale,
even black and white,
harlequin pork chops
but we make no such distinctions
because we are all pigs.
To other pigs I am attractive, desirable,
for that's what leads to the making of other pigs,
attraction, desire.
Mud and squalor are the best,
they are my perfume,
my scented water.
Like Cleopatra with a snout
the sweet milk of decay laps over me.
Although some of you feed off us
we are not a popular race;
we are a term of abuse.
We are referred to when bad table manners are prevalent
we are used to describe selfish, opinionated
masculine humans who are scornful of women.
And many have written ill of us
especially vegetarians, George Orwell and religion.
Our best time is when we're young
with our cute little tails
and squeaky snorts
when we get older and slower
the reviews become cruel and personal.
However, where there is poverty we adapt,
pigs don't have weight problems
we get fat anywhere.

CHRISTMAS BONUS – MAGNIFICAT

My soul magnifies the poor
the sore
the raw
and my spirit rejoices in God
my downcast
my outcast
my twig-bone wrong caste
for He regards the low estate
the no-go estate
the empty plate
and squats there with those generations.

For at Whose Name the Cosmos shakes
and canyons quake
sought sanctuary within a womb
a young girl's chaste, unopened room
a sparse, unblemished catacomb
and holy is He amongst the lame.

His mercy is on those who fear Him
hear Him
those near Him
in desert flapping bivouac or dehydrated barrio.

The night sky rolled out by His arm,
the preening proud ignore His balm
and slink towards the warlock charm
of their small ambitions;
and those on thrones end up alone
replaced by fly-pecked innocents.

He only eats with the hungry,
and if they don't, He too refrains;
and as for the rich –
a table can not be found for them.

My soul magnifies the poor
the sore
the raw
and my spirit rejoices in God
my outcast.

JESUS, JEWEL OF THE POOR

From the crystal courts of Heaven
to the fly-blown stable floor
This a different kind of glory
Jesus, jewel of the poor.

Visionary of unknown planets
strolls unnoticed by the shore
This a sparse and modest glory
Jesus, jewel of the poor.

Made the dust walk by His breathing
weeping image of the Law
This a strangely chosen glory
Jesus, jewel of the poor.

Zeal of Heaven hangs exhausted,
bore the gouge of Satan's claw
This a beaten, hopeless glory
Jesus, jewel of the poor.

Homeless Saviour of the nomad
lifts the starving through His door
This the just and finished glory
Jesus, jewel of the poor.

FAT WOMAN ON THE SOFA

FAT WOMAN ON THE SOFA

Introduction

Fat Woman was born
nobody clapped
she was never chained up
but perpetually trapped
Fat Woman lived
and wanted to die
Fat Woman hurt
and didn't know why

FAT WOMAN ON THE SOFA

Nobody will listen to Fat Woman,
she sits spread over
cushions and exact covers
asking things;
and her words disappear
like breath,
so she doubts she said them.

From within her shape
she hears high thoughts,
and once when love
left her
for someone thinner
she wrote weakly on a
steamed window
'We lived
 Then we died
 of natural causes'
but being Fat Woman
it was
not published

FAT WOMAN IN THE HALL OF MIRRORS

Fat Woman inspects her body
it grieves her
there is too much of it
She thinks she resembles a gross, wild mushroom,
a mutant mound
bulging in the dainty glade of life

Moving to another mirror
she sees a new image
where she appears inside out;
she no longer
a thyroid soufflé
but a small, shimmering prism
from which shines
cones of colour
that search the sky
for new planets and exploding stars.
And through her gossamer rays
a jubilee of luminous leaves
race and roll
speaking of their genesis

Fat Woman lingers at this place
realising there were never any
friendly mirrors,
only her emotions
and some of them were
heavily padded.

FAT WOMAN AND THE PURVEYORS
OF GOD

As usual, Fat Woman had a few queries,
such as
When God sculpted the female breast
who was he thinking of?
This speculation, for that's all it was,
was considered rather unclean
in some circles and not for study,
certainly not on your own.
'Things happen when you're on your own'
Fat Woman was told,
'when you're lonely.
So stay in groups
and be personable.'
Others thought Fat Woman's conjecture
quite clownish.
'What an individual you are.
We've never had one like you before.
You're just like us.
You're very novel.
Sing this . . . and let's see you dance.'
Conscious of her size
but grateful for this initial acceptance
Fat Woman jigged awkwardly
and when asked
what she thought of it all, replied:
'Well it seems to me that we're in
the presence of a maxim
addicted to jingles
and much warmed by sentiment.'
That was it. Fat Woman had said

the wrong thing again.
Her latest thoughts were regarded
as offensive and very hurtful
to large numbers of people,
'and the door's over there'.

Yearning the solace and substance of mystery
Fat Woman walked away and imagined
an owl quartering in the mists of
her nesting worlds.

Before the task of sleep
Fat Woman asked nobody
if God had perfect breasts,
or even feathers?

FAT WOMAN EXCOMMUNICATED

Fat Woman overhears a conversation.
At the seat of power
the Purveyors of God are discussing her.
'She's loud
and very unsound.
So sad for one
who hogs the spotlight.
Because of her arrogance
she always wants to take over.
It is right we didn't give in to her, if we had
she would, no doubt, have removed us
and then what would have happened to our dreams?
She is unstable and far from whole,
constantly jostling for a place
which was never there for her anyway.
It was right we took action
against those unhealthy needs.
Such tragedy in one so huge.
We will be seen to be right.
Besides, we could never use her,
she's too fat.'

Fat Woman cannot recognise herself
in the things they say;
but assumes they must be right,
as they are the Purveyors of God.
Inside her, all is so different;
there are butterflies and kingfishers
tulips
and tenderness
where none are turned away.

Fat Woman wants to cry out
from behind whatever it is they think they see
'Look at me'
'Listen to me'
'Deep in me is that which is holy'.

Instead, Fat Woman gets fatter
and in so doing
becomes invisible.

FAT WOMAN'S TUNE

Fat Woman has a tune
it's something she made up
between elation and winter.
She thinks it says something about her
and needing friendship
she showed it to some people

They added their own bits
and soon it ceased to be hers
Transposed, as it was,
into a different key.
Not hers any more
but she pretends it is.

FAT WOMAN CHANGING

Fat Woman curls up and howls
not loudly, because of the neighbours,
but inside the way the bereaved often do
The noise has gone on for years
even when she sleeps
Lately, the pitch has changed
and curiously
the noise has begun to speak
Fat Woman lies still and listens
and, in time, is visited
by the priest of dreams.

FAT WOMAN DREAMS

I'm going back into the Kingdom of Can't
in order to cause a revolt
I'm growing these wings of deliberate strength
magnificent spans that won't moult

I'm going back into the Kingdom of Can't
to gather up bonfires of hope
I'm ready to burn up the heaps of the past
and silence the tongue of 'can't cope'

I'm going back into the Kingdom of Can't
to prise open tombs of regret
I'm crying out loud like an exorcised soul
I'm a pauper delivered from debt

I'm going back into the Kingdom of Can't
with a body of marble and mink
and there I'll unleash that most terrible beast
Fat Woman-starting-to-think

FAT WOMAN'S LOVE

Something is happening to Fat Woman
far beyond that which she expected
Someone has begun to love her
This person has held her
stroked her
and whispered eternal things

She is not sure why this should be
and though this love
speaks a fragile language
Fat Woman, in response,
is becoming the impossible –
a flower growing on an iceberg
a peep of gloss petals
even bees are now crossing the frozen ocean
such is the richness of her pollen

Fat Woman has become summer
fertile,
bright,
full-blazing
in a place where there should have been
none

And love
is making her
boast into being

FAT WOMAN ON THE SOFA

Benediction

Fat Woman has not ended
she's not too stout to run
This morning is her morning
Fat Woman has begun . . .